IRIS APFEL

A Little Golden Book® Biography

T0354260

By Deborah Blumenthal

Illustrated by Ellen Surrey

A GOLDEN BOOK • NEW YORK

Educators and librarians, for a variety of teaching tools, visit us at RHTeachersLibrarians.com
Library of Congress Control Number: 2022947566
ISBN 978-0-593-64376-1 (trade) — ISBN 978-0-593-64377-8 (ebook)
Printed in the United States of America
10 9 8 7 6 5 4 3 2 1

Iris Apfel is a businesswoman, an interior designer, and a fashion icon.

Iris Barrel (Apfel) was born on August 29, 1921, and raised on a farm in Astoria, Queens (when Astoria still had farms!).

Iris was an only child. Her dad owned a mirror-and-glass company. Her mom owned a fashion boutique. Iris loved watching how her mom transformed simple daytime outfits into fancy evening wear, using jewelry, scarves, bags, and shoes. Iris learned how she could show her personality through the clothes and accessories she wore, like the giant eyeglasses that later made her famous.

Iris always knew what she liked when it came to fashion. One day when she was about four, Iris and her parents were at an elegant hotel. Iris's mother was dressing her to go out. As her mom put a ribbon in her hair, Iris began to shriek. Was she hurt? No. The ribbon didn't match her outfit, and that was unacceptable to Iris!

Iris's interest in art and design began when she was a little girl visiting her grandparents in Brooklyn. Her grandma had bags of fabric scraps that she kept in her closet. Iris would spill them out and sit on the floor studying them like a jeweler examining rare gems. She was fascinated by all the different patterns, colors, and textures, grouping the samples that went together best.

When it was time to go home, her grandma let her pick out six samples she could take with her. Iris didn't know it at the time, but all that fun with fabrics would help her become a fabric expert later in life.

Iris's mom, who always dressed beautifully, was her fashion role model—although, Iris said, her mom's style of dressing "was quite different" from hers. Still, Iris never forgot her mom's most important bit of fashion advice: Invest in a few basic pieces of fine clothing—like a little black dress—and spend the rest of your money on accessories.

When Iris was twelve, she began buying her own clothes. It was 1933, and she needed an outfit for the Easter Parade on Fifth Avenue. Her mom was too busy working to take her shopping, so Iris tucked the twenty-five dollars that her parents gave her into her bag and, all alone, headed to Manhattan.

She bought not only a dress but also shoes and a straw hat, leaving enough money for lunch and the five-cent subway ride home. Her parents approved. And so began her career as an expert shopper!

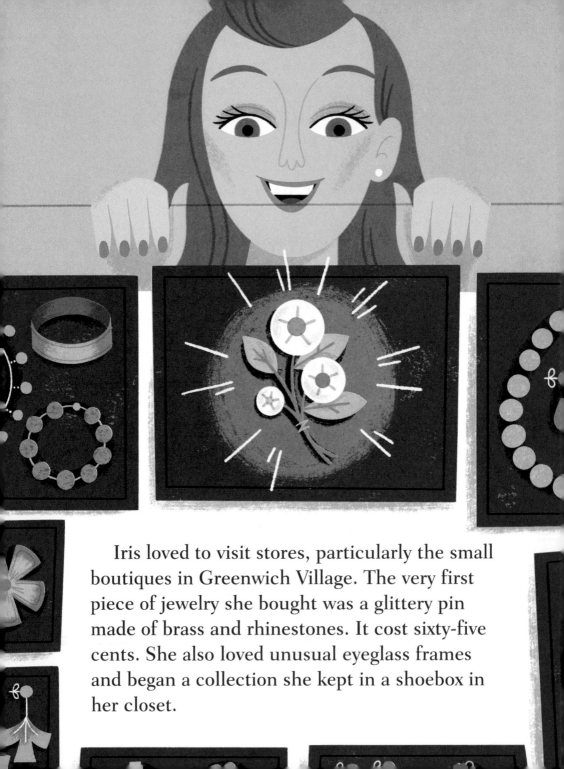

Iris loved to visit stores, particularly the small boutiques in Greenwich Village. The very first piece of jewelry she bought was a glittery pin made of brass and rhinestones. It cost sixty-five cents. She also loved unusual eyeglass frames and began a collection she kept in a shoebox in her closet.

Iris later studied art history at New York University and went to art school at the University of Wisconsin. In 1948, while on vacation at Lake George in New York, she met a man named Carl Apfel. They fell in love and married within a few months.

Iris and Carl started a textile and design company in 1950 and kept the company for over forty years, until they retired. They had many famous clients and selected fabrics and restored furniture for the White House for nine presidents: Harry Truman, Dwight Eisenhower, John F. Kennedy, Lyndon Johnson, Richard Nixon, Gerald Ford, Jimmy Carter, Ronald Reagan, and Bill Clinton.

While Iris and Carl traveled the world to buy textiles, Iris continued to buy clothes and accessories.

Iris thought of life as a celebration and loved to dress up. When the time came for her to finally need glasses, Iris wanted to have fun with them and had lenses put into her BIG frames.

And bracelets? While other people put on one bracelet or two, Iris covered her arms with them, some expensive and some from flea markets. She also wore layers of necklaces in every length. It took her hours to get dressed. But when she did, people noticed!

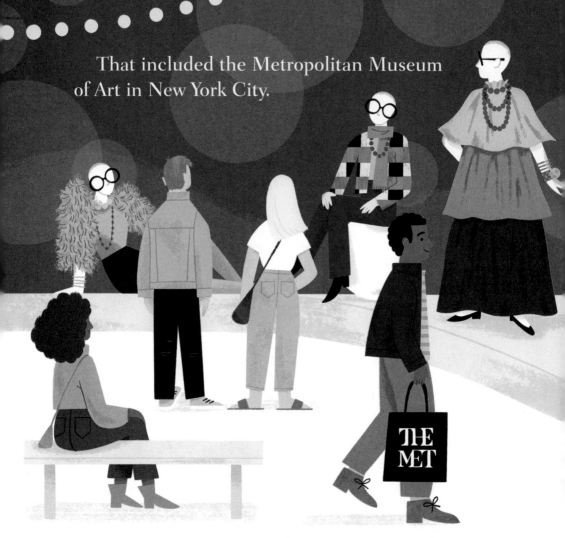

That included the Metropolitan Museum of Art in New York City.

In 2005, after a show got canceled, the museum called her asking if they could quickly put together a "small" exhibit about her unique style. They called the show *Rara Avis: Selections from the Iris Apfel Collection.* "Rara Avis" means "rare bird," because Iris *was* an unusual woman.

The show ended up being BIG, with more than eighty outfits and hundreds of accessories. It was so popular it launched her fashion career. New York made her famous, Iris said, so she called herself "the geriatric starlet." ("Geriatric" refers to someone who's older.)

Age never stopped Iris. At ninety, she worked with a cosmetics company to develop lipsticks, nail polishes, and eye shadows. When she was ninety-six, the company that made Barbie dolls created an Iris Apfel Barbie! And at ninety-seven, Iris signed a modeling contract.

Iris and Carl were married for sixty-seven years. Carl died three days before his 101st birthday, on August 1, 2015.

Iris lives in New York City and in Palm Beach, Florida. She has a jewelry line and a line of eyeglasses. She teaches. There's even a movie about her.

On August 21, 2021, Iris celebrated her one hundredth birthday. But Iris doesn't act old. She likes to go out and have fun. She describes herself as the world's oldest living teenager.

Iris loves jazz and lives life the way jazz musicians play music: try this, try that, with nothing carefully planned. Wherever she goes, people recognize her. Wearing her big glasses, bright lipstick, and bold outfits, Iris dazzles the world with her special gift—her own colorful style.